thoughts spoken from the heart

Over 500 thoughts that bring meaning to your life

LOLLY DASKAL

Printed in the United States of America

Lead From Within Publishing

ISBN-13: 978-0615909431
ISBN-10: 0615909434

Book design by Carrie Ralston, Simple Girl Design LLC

To Michaele, Ariel, and Zoe

*My three beloved children who have shown me
the hidden power of my heart.*

introduction

We are all travelers who serendipitously buy tickets for a trip through life, never quite knowing where the journey will ultimately take us.

The final destination is determined, in part, by mysterious forces and the choices that we make throughout our lives.

Only after we arrive at our destination, shake off the dust, and look back at the distance traveled can we truly recognize that it all made perfect sense.

I cannot say where my journey will lead me but, like most of us, I am wiser now than when I began. I hope this book brings you some valuable life lessons to accompany you on your life's journey.

I hope you will view this book as your gentle companion — your fellow traveler in exploring your heart.

These thoughts spoken from the heart will provide you with a key to unlock your inner wisdom. The most crucial ingredient for our journey is introspection, and even simple thoughts have the power to bring meaning to our lives. Feel free to read this book cover to cover or randomly dip into it. Make sure to reflect, question, or act on each thought. My hope is that each thought will provide you with a meaningful perspective of yourself and the world around you.

As a person who is immersed in all aspects of the heart, I have found that our mental attitude is the most influential factor in the search for meaningfulness.

In order to change conditions outside us, we must first change within.

Our heart is the key.

Leading from the heart is the way I live my life. It saved me through rough patches in my life, such as homelessness, divorce, single motherhood, and grave illness.

By leading from within, you can face difficulties with calm and reason while keeping peace within yourself.

These thoughts can open the door to profound knowledge of the workings of our mind and nature of our heart.

Our heart's thoughts are the trustworthy couriers of our soul.

There is only a fine line that separates who we are from whom we want to be. And as Carl Jung's teachings show us, we must honor the self, so the self will honor us. If we ignore the self, it will leave us to our own devices, but if we cultivate a relationship with self and our inner wisdom, by listening to our intuition and our heart, it will fill us with new insight and help us reach our potential.

However difficult or lonely our lives may seem at times, if we surrender ourselves to the possibilities that lie within our heart, clarity will eventually emerge. There is no jumping over obstacles in life, only digging deeper to overcome them.

Although we may feel lost at times or allow ourselves to become hijacked by debilitating thoughts, we can always return home — to the heart — which keeps us on our true path in life, guiding us to its secret destination.

May these thoughts help you realize your innermost dreams. May they put your thoughts into words and send an echo though your bones. May you wake up one morning and say, "I have found meaning in my life."

If even one of my thoughts touches your heart, if it inspires you to find your life's calling, if it helps you to connect with another, then my purpose has been fulfilled.

As you read this book, know these thoughts are my way of giving back to you, with a warm feeling of gratitude and companionship for those on the journey alongside me, and I return my thoughts to you with heart.

AT THE CENTER

HEART

OF LIFE IS YOUR

There is a big difference between
being centered and being self-centered.

Be willing to take a stand for the things
you believe in, because no one else
will stand there for you.

Where we fall are the stepping stones
for our journey.

We must be willing to take chances
to see the artistry of our transformation.

Purpose drives the process through which we become what we are capable of being.

Choose the dreams that are important to you and the ones that touch your heart.

Appreciate people for who they are, and for who they are not.

Change what you can change; embrace what you can't change.

There is no significance in life without struggle.

There are no limitations
except those we create for ourselves.

Put yourself in a position where you have to
stretch your comfort zone, because that is
where you will engage your heart.

Longing for purpose is longing for meaning.

Before trying to change anyone,
first seek change within yourself.

Love yourself unconditionally, faults and all.

Most of us will do anything
to avoid facing ourselves.

Your purpose will become clear
only when you listen to your heart.

we **become** what we **believe.**

Knowing our own demons is the best way
to understand the darkness of others.

Wisdom lies within both truth and error.

Often the heart will solve the problem
that the mind has struggled with in vain.

Unless you change the way you see things,
they will remain the same.

Never pretend you understand what is happening with the mind alone. We must listen to our heart to truly understand.

Point directly at your own heart, and you will find your purpose.

When you plant a seed in the ground, don't keep digging it up to see if it's growing.

Make gratitude a habit.

Serenity means not having to change anything
about the present.

Know that compassion for others
begins with accepting and forgiving yourself.

You have all the wisdom and strength
that you need within you.

Learn from failure and experiment around it.

Being grateful connects us to the joy and riches
that we have in our lives.

Many of us do not listen to ourselves
deeply enough to know how we feel.

Realize the incredible power of your heart
to shape your life.

Coincidences can become meaningful
opportunities for creativity.

LISTENING IS A HUMAN ELEMENT.

Caring is a human essential.

Each one of us is the hero
of our own life's story.

In all disorder there is order.

To create more abundance,
banish any thought that you are a failure.

Make relationships and love your number one
priority and you will be wealthy.

How we look at something may not be
the same thing as how it actually is.

You cannot love anyone if you hate yourself.

Sometimes we repeat the same patterns
day after day, while our heart is calling us
to do something meaningful and different.

Experience teaches us what we can
and cannot do.

Always keep defining who you are, where you are, and where you want to be in life.

You are not your thoughts.

The past is who I have been
and the future is who I will become.
Concentrate on who you are right now.

Sometimes we hang onto thoughts
that are as stale as old bread.

We don't see the world as it is;
we see it through our own lens.

Success is never a one-shot deal.

Our minds tend to take everything literally and,
before you know it, our words become truths.

Love builds bridges. Fear builds swamps.

A BAD ATTITUDE IS

CONTAGIOUS

Values are revealed when times are toughest.

Earn the right to hold others to high standards
by meeting them yourself.

Our emotions are not who we are.

Recognize when to stop fixing
and realize when to just let it be.

Confusion abounds when we do not like
the answer we are given.

Imagination is more important than wisdom,
because imagination encompasses
the limitless universe.

Less is more, simple is better,
and action is imperative.

We can easily sabotage ourselves
if we don't believe we deserve success.

Do not allow your fear to feed on itself.

Who you are on the inside should match
who you are on the outside.

The future is not ours to see,
but it is ours to create.

We can't be there until we are here.

Ability without determination is futile.

Patience is the pace of the heart
speaking to us slowly.

Our values have their own rewards.

Never compromise your values;
they are the stamp of your heart.

TO HAVE AN

OPEN MIND,

WE NEED TO

EXPAND

OUR HEART.

Passion stretches us and gives our life meaning.

Words are the building blocks of thoughts.

It hurts when other people reject us;
it hurts even more when we reject ourselves.

Recognize when to stop talking
and realize when to start listening.

Travel this journey baggage-free.

Sometimes we need help making peace
with ourselves.

Integrity is the sum of who you are.

During times of change, we know who we have
been, but not who we're becoming.

The purpose of our heart is to understand
and to seek.

We create our own meaning of life as we go.

Each one of us has our own personal puzzle to
create and solve.

We can weather anything if we stay calm
in the eye of the storm.

Recognize when to stop overacting
and realize when to start reflecting.

A goal is a dream with a deadline.

Both pain and joy shape us as a person.

Without a purpose that is bigger than yourself,
you are more likely to serve only yourself.

we do not

g r o w

our lives; we

create

our lives.

Being loud does not mean being confident.

Listen to the voice of your heart
and what it is saying.

To confront your own shadow
is to shine light on your own greatness.

When you locate the voice of the heart, trust it.

Confusion exists when the mind is speaking
and the heart does not agree.

Don't inflict pains from your past
on your present relationships.

Look beyond your problems —
solutions are everywhere.

Have patience with everything
that goes unanswered by your heart.

Sometimes we just need to experience life
without questioning everything.

Approach each challenge with an attitude
that there's something to learn.

Never lower your standards.

The more technology we produce,
the more we ache for human touch.

Trust what you know,
not what you think you know.

Instead of waiting for confidence, act as if the
change you desire has already taken place.

Shine a light on your dark days.

Power and strength are great, but we are more
beautiful when we are vulnerable and human.

Sometimes our thoughts are like paperweights — they hold us down.

The secret to being happy is to
cultivate an attitude of gratitude.

Your heart is the place where you find yourself
again and again.

Live by the inner rapture of your values.

To the soul there is no distinction
between giving and receiving.

We only have one life to live.
Choose your values carefully.

We are here to make a difference and mend
the fractures of the world, one act at a time.

Say yes to life and go and fight for it.

Go inward and discover heart;
go outward and discover your gifts.

Some of us have learned to protect ourselves
by caring for others, while refusing to let love
into our own lives.

People who would never verbally abuse another
do it to themselves every day.

To be who we are and to become
what we are capable of becoming
is all that is expected of us.

The present moment is where feelings are felt,
decisions are made, and change is possible.

The process of achievement comes through
repeated failures and the constant need
to do better.

Sometimes the little steps can add up to a lot.

Just because you think it, does not make it so.

Lonely people build walls around themselves
and then wonder why they can't be seen.

What I seek

I shall

FIND.

Opposition can become our greatest teacher;
a good challenge can bring out our best.

Vulnerability is the new strong.

We are all worthy and none of us
is dispensable.

Every person I meet has something to teach me.

All suffering is a doorway, all pain is an entrance,
and all loss is a gate.

Love is difficult to learn if not experienced.

Moving in the direction of our dreams
moves us toward our destiny.

We are led safely by the messages from within,
the people we meet,
and circumstances we encounter.

Knowledge gives capability, wisdom provides
orientation, and ambition is the fire
that sparks the way.

Wherever you go, take yourself with you.

Success is measured by how many hearts
you have touched.

When we lead from fear, we erode trust.

When we unite wisdom with knowledge,
we reach our potential.

If you need help, look within first.

We must know our own happiness, and
we must bear the suffering of our wounds.

Most of us are so externally focused
that we rarely have the time to venture inward.

WHEN WE INQUIRE, WE DREAM.

WHEN WE ARE CURIOUS, WE LEARN.

Courage removes obstacles in our way.

Fear is a wonderful teacher and a lousy master.

Some people will be successful, some people
will hope to be successful, and others
will be prepared to not succeed.

You will never win by fooling yourself.

Until we're aware of the unconscious patterns responsible for our choices, we cannot expect change in our lives.

There is no failure in losing, only in quitting.

Happiness is not gained from outward manifestation; it is gained from who we are on the inside.

Trust is fragile, yet crucial to any relationship.

Every circumstance, at every given moment, calls out for the right action.

A lack of clarity and alignment with self creates confusion and chaos.

There is always a way from where you are to where you want to go.

We create our own armor to protect us from the things we fear most.

Wanting is the beginning of our journey,
getting is the destination,
and there is a lot of traveling in between.

The most important thing to learn is how to listen.

It takes more effort to cultivate your strengths
than to hide your weaknesses.

No one was born to lead
and no one was born to follow.

The greatest leaders are those who **empower others** without them knowing it.

You cannot share what you do not feel.

It is so easy to look around and see
what is wrong, but it takes good practice
to see what is right.

Negativity is powerful;
it empowers the problem.

Walk in the footsteps of those you admire.

Trust is a strong chain, but difficult to repair once broken.

To the courageous heart, nothing is impossible.

Be the person who brings a little magic to other people's moments.

Fear is an element of progress.

Those who have a hard time changing their
minds are usually the ones who have
a hard time accepting anything.

The most important trust issue that we face
is learning to trust ourselves.

Intuition is ever present for those
who have a heart to feel it.

Trust takes time to develop;
it is easy to lose and harder to regain.

To rebuild trust, we must understand
the importance of trust.

We should know what our convictions are
and stand firmly for them.

Being controlling comes from feeling powerless.

If you never admit you made a mistake,
how will you learn from failure?

WHAT WE CANNOT
FACE OR EXPRESS

ACTIONS
SPEAKS THROUGH OUR
ACTIONS.

Turn negative complaints into positive
aspirations — move from *I don't* to *I do*.

Learn how to shift your focus from being
successful to being significant.

People rise to our expectations.

People are lonely because they build walls
instead of bridges.

We have a tendency to adopt the attitudes
of those we spend time with.

Be willing to trust your heart and
listen to the voice of your soul.

The price of greatness is accountability.

The things we spend most of our time pursuing
turn out to be what we find important.

Wisdom is profound only when it's understood.

Ego keeps us playing small in life.

When things go wrong, have faith that everything is going according to plan.

Perfectionism is often hiding in the shadows of those who fall under the influence of fear.

Find your passion and your purpose will follow.

Don't be afraid of the fire in your heart.

Passion is the secret to many success stories.

It can be easier to go numb and not feel
than to feel and be alive.

THE MIND TAKES THINGS

a p a r t

TO SEE HOW THEY WORK;

THE HEART PUTS THINGS

together

TO SEE WHAT THEY MEAN.

Sometimes the easiest thing to give is money,
and the hardest thing to give is heart.

Trust is the glue that binds relationships together.

Struggles happen at important junctures
in our lives.

The person we neglect when we give too much
is usually ourself.

Boundaries are about saying no;
they reflect what we believe we deserve.

Imitate the successes of the wise
and not the mistakes of fools.

Ambition knows no moderation.

Keep kindness in your heart.

Empowerment is oxygen to the soul.

The next time you find yourself in conflict,
instead of seeing who is right and
who is wrong, find common ground.

Purpose provides direction.

Manage change — do not let it manage you.

Reach for the unreachable.

Let the passion of what you want to become
be greater than the fear of becoming it.

Success is failure turned inside out.

Holding onto the past keeps it alive
and gives it power in the present.

our struggles braid the

mind&heart

to pull us deeper into ourselves.

Being happy is a choice, but it takes
constant effort to make it happen.

When we accept help from others,
it allows them to feel close to us.

Avoiding a thought does not make it go away.

Learn by teaching.

Stop believing everything you think.

The future is not a place we are going,
but a place we are creating.

The more you know what's right for you,
the easier it is to say that something
does not feel right.

True confidence stems from self-reflection.

Nothing comes to a dreamer but dreams.

Our years teach us to have patience.
Hindsight is insight.

Life takes on meaning
when you live your purpose.

At the heart of genuine humility
is never forgetting who you are,
no matter where you are.

Focus on creating a journey of meaning.

Do one thing each day that is of service
to someone else.

We all need a deep-rooted purpose,
so that when things fall apart,
we can stand up with courage.

Passion comes from the heart, not the mind.

Creativity is the

intersection

of the known and the unknown.

Put your heart into everything you do.

Self-confidence is not about the impression
you give to other people,
but who you are on the inside.

Seek the truth, even though it may be painful.

Don't think anything about yourself
that you don't want to come true.

Never compare yourself to someone else.
You never really know their life
behind closed doors.

Deep listening mean more than hearing
with our ears.

It's wonderful to always be doing,
but don't forget to *be* your best.

It takes courage to be yourself.

The deeper you dig,
the more connected you feel.

Gifts and talents are given *to* us,
but value is created *by* us.

We can climb the highest mountains
and we can navigate the darkest valleys,
but we cannot do it all at once.

Our values color our perspective.

Humanity is born out of the heart's revelation
that another person is every bit
as important as we are.

Nothing is impossible with an open heart.

The heart knows when the mind struggles.

Tiny changes can add up to big differences.

whatever you do,
do it with
heart.

There has to be room in life
for something bigger than ourselves,
and larger than self-interest.

Life is change and change is life.

Welcome traveling companions
on your journey through life.

When we take ownership for what happens
in life, we are empowered to make
the necessary changes.

The difference between impossible and possible
is a willing heart.

Words are x-rays of our heart,
a connection between our inner self
and the world around us.

All limits are self-inflicted.

You can find some failure in every success story.

Experience is a great teacher.

You are not your labels.
You are not your failures.
You are simply you.

If it is worth doing, it is worth doing well.

When walking the tightrope of challenges, meet
yourself halfway and lead yourself to safety.

The greatest war within each individual
is between the head and the heart.

The unmasking of ego is getting to
the heart of what matters.

Our values define what we stand for
and what we tolerate.

Expectations create an intense gap
between what is and what will be.

BE THE
LEADER
YOU WANT TO
SEE
IN THE
WORLD.

Many times we do things because
we want to be accepted, but all we are doing
is cheating ourselves from our greatness.

It's okay to say *I have failed*.

It's okay to ask for help.

Solutions are always in the room,
waiting to be summoned.

Sometimes we never know what we're
looking for until we find it.

The hardest part of letting go
is remembering to do it.

It's hard to have patience when we're not sure
we're going to get what we're waiting for.

Surrender your control
and get out of your own way.

Sometimes patience hurts, but the consequence of not having patience hurts even more.

Courage is refusing to be a slave to fear.

The magic of today is in the moment.

Your mind is about survival;
your heart is about surrender.

Being present breeds gratitude.

Live life with passion and an open heart.

Pain is not an abnormal condition;
it is nature's way of healing the heart.

Knowing we can protect ourselves
plays a big part in being authentic.

LEADING FROM

within

IS LEADING

FROM THE

heart.

Your presence is hereby requested in your life.

Shutting down is a protective response to pain.

The heart yearns to be appreciated.

Fear of rejection keeps us stuck
in our own trepidation.

A broken heart that is put together
is a work of art.

Patience is not a virtue; it is an achievement.

If your life does not feel right, it is your prerogative
to create something better for yourself.

When you are busy looking over your shoulder,
you lose sight of yourself.

Studying the past can help us
lead in the present.

Trust is contagious.

Most of our problems come from not telling
ourselves the truth about ourselves.

Follow your heart and
have the courage to dream.

Even confident people have limiting beliefs about themselves.

The hardest thing about a personal storm is that we don't know how to protect ourselves.

Negativity breeds negativity.

Fear of change immobilizes the potential for greatness.

Many of us have learned

TOLERANCE

around

INTOLERANT

people.

Waiting for things to change
will not make change happen.

For every point of clarity
there is some confusion.

Don't make *your* challenges
the challenges of *others*.

What will you do today
to impact your tomorrow?

The greatest gift you can give someone
is your full attention.

Taming our personality does not mean
we are breaking our spirit.

We are most alive when we are learning,
creating, and discovering.

When we're no longer able to change a situation,
we are challenged to change ourselves.

Behaviors that get reinforced get repeated.

When you lose your direction,
look inside to find yourself.

Slowing down allows us to realize that life
is about progress, not perfection.

Listen to the spaces between the words.

To be in the company of another
is to be alone together.

When you find yourself in a challenging state,
take the time to breathe.

Do not waste any more time.
Live the life you were meant to live.

Emotions are important signals for action.

BEFORE I CAN DO,

I MUST **BE.**

The hardest thing about practicing patience
is being patient.

The hidden power of the heart is love.

Authenticity is the narrative of our truth.

Life waits for us on the other side of our ego.

Our values are revealed
when times are toughest.

Think of something you want and take
the first steps toward making it happen.

Don't allow others to be the darkness
that overshadows your brightness.

Express what you want and see if you get
what you need.

The mind is about fragmentation
and the heart is about making it whole.

If you are not interested, nothing is interesting.

Integrity is the result of trust in one's life.

Control is an illusion and uncertainty
is the reality.

Life beckons us to take charge of our destiny
and be accountable for our actions.

In this life, you get what you give.

Your mind likes to spend time figuring things out;
your heart goes straight to the matter.

Having a connection to our work
brings our heart to what we do.

TRUST YOUR HEART LIKE YOUR LIFE DEPENDS ON IT.

The choice is ours whether to continue
on the same path or engage the future.

The heart always feels
before the mind can think.

Recognize when to stop leading
and realize when to start including.

Trust makes the heart grow fonder.

What gets recognized gets reinforced.

The mind should always remain ajar,
ready to experience the heart.

Life is about determining how much risk
we are willing to take to find a deeper meaning
within ourselves.

Life is a chain of repeated acts of trust.

Defensiveness might seem like protection,
but it pushes people away.

Trust the wisdom of failure.

Sometimes we expect those we love to make up
for something we can't give ourselves.

We are in trouble when we try to change others
to please ourselves.

Love grows best when we accept differences
without forcing change.

Constant hurrying can be used to escape
and anesthetize our real feelings.

Listening means more than
hearing people's words.

Without vision we lose sight of the future
and remain stuck in the past.

IN THE STILLING

OF OUR STRUGGLE

WE FIND SOLACE

IN OUR LIVING.

Hindsight is where we've been.
Foresight is what is in front of us.
Insight is the view from within.

We cannot move through our fears
until we realize we are afraid.

If you take action only on the days
you feel good, not much will get done.

When we are inspired by some great purpose,
we transcend our limitations.

In challenging times, remember that pain is real
but struggle is optional.

Make people feel they are the heart
of what is important.

A person of integrity faces the music
even when they don't like the tune.

Your character shapes your life.
Your attitude shapes your actions.
Your actions shape your direction.

A thought can only come true
if it is linked to behavior.

The biggest pitfall in our lives develops
when we do not honor who we are.

It's easy to let negative thoughts
spiral out of control.

When you look for the good in others,
they reveal themselves to you.

We are drowning in information
but starved for knowledge.

When you are aware of self, you can lead others.

Our values tell other people
how they will be treated.

You cannot believe everything you think.

FEAR

is the voice of the rational mind.

There are always breakdowns
before breakthroughs.

Suffering ceases to be suffering
at the moment it finds meaning.

Our heart sets things straight, giving us
a sense of our true priorities.

Owning something also means
owning up to something.

Consistency and continuity are another way
of saying you can trust me.

Problems are gifts in our lives.
They make us stretch out of our comfort zone.

We can never be bored as long as we are
in love with life.

Accepting responsibility means
you respond with your best ability.

Do not confuse envy with desire.

Make what matters, really matter.

Owning our story can be hard,
but not nearly as difficult as
spending our lives running from it.

Write your story with the narrative
of your heart.

Life is not only about strength and gifts;
it is also about liabilities and limits.

We give ourselves a gift when we
trust ourselves with others.

Make your values your guiding star for life.

Our struggles are to our life what exercise
is to muscle; they toughen us up
and make us stronger.

you must
commit to
do whatever
it takes to be
more.

Intuition is hard to explain,
but it shows the way.

Say yes to sorrow, then go and defeat it.

Our heart is more than a pump.
It is the lifeline to our purpose.

Compassion is to the heart
what oxygen is to the body.

The heart is the seat of emotions
and the gut of our feelings.

The heart is the seed of humanity.

Wisdom is knowing what to do next;
knowledge is knowing how to make it happen.

Sometimes loving yourself means
accepting yourself.

The heart weeps the tears that the mind
refuses to acknowledge.

If you believe in something,
leave no room for doubt.

When everything seems to be going
against you, remember that an airplane
takes off against the wind.

The right word at the right time
can change a life.

Change is required for self-preservation.

The mystery of this moment is that it makes possible all the moments to come.

Experience this moment with the heart and allow the mind to take care of the future.

Trust your heart to make your life choices.

We are all poems in search of a

VOICE.

Our humility brings us closer to
what our heart is longing for us to be.

All humans are in search of meaning.

Self-acceptance is making peace with yourself.

We cannot move through our fears
until we realize we are afraid.

When we rely on the mind, we are seeking to make sense. When we rely on the heart, things just make sense.

The heart has nothing to prove; it simply reveals.

Sometimes we hold onto negative thoughts as though our life depended on it.

People may doubt what you say, but they will believe what you do.

Stop talking about how things used to be and start talking about how things will be.

Say yes to beauty and go and admire it.

Avoid telling people what they want to hear. Instead, tell them what they need to hear.

Make every mistake a learning opportunity.

There is a value to words that goes
far beyond their meaning.

Courage is the choice to be vulnerable.

The ability to know your feelings makes
effective communication much more likely.

Many of us don't appreciate
that our lives are shaped by tiny moments
strung together by choice.

find new ways of doing
Old Things.

We cannot control what happens to us,
but we can control our choices.

Our values tie our heart and mind together.

Listen to what people say
and then watch what they do.

Leave everybody you encounter
better for having met you.

Post change…don't postpone change.

Saying *I understand*
doesn't necessarily mean you agree.

You reach new realms of happiness when you
thank those who have impacted you.

Let nature be your teacher.
Let experience be your guide.

Listen with the ears of your soul.

Recognize when to stop rescuing
and realize when to let it fail.

How you think is a by-product of
how self-confident you feel.

If you continue doing what you have always
done, you will continue to get the same results.

You cannot have rewards without risks.

Be selfish — never share the blame
for your mistakes.

Insight alone does not cause change.
Change requires action.

Sometimes you have to lose yourself
to find yourself.

There is a big difference
between knowing yourself

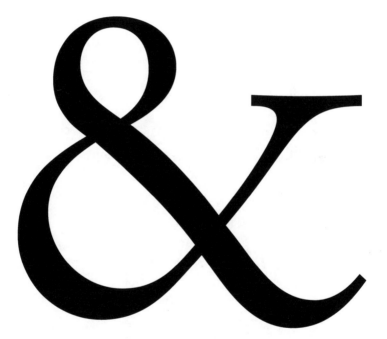

**UNDERSTANDING
YOURSELF.**

Model the behavior you want to see in others.

Live for today and plan for tomorrow.

If you always do what you've always done,
you will always get what you've always gotten.

Recognize when to stop regretting
and realize when to start appreciating.

If you don't know something, admit it.

You can always move forward
if you have a change of heart.

Everything impossible can become
a possible miracle.

Nothing is more valuable then becoming
the person you are meant to be.

Become more conscious of your feelings
and how they translate into thoughts.

Examine your thoughts
and explore all your options.

Repeated patterns show our weakness
from within.

Our values lead us to our greater purpose.

Relieve yourself from the need to judge;
it causes a conversation of right and wrong.

Judgment creates separation;
it is ego's form of defensiveness.

The walls that we build to keep other people
away also keep others from entering.

Recognize when to stop deciding
and realize when to start discussing.

THE GREATEST BRUISES DO NOT EVEN LEAVE A MARK ON THE SKIN.

What we choose becomes our life.

Give back more than you have been given.

Many of us confuse love with approval
and leadership with power.

Life is best defined by trial and error.

Self-worth opens many doors.

Operating from your purpose is not only about
what you do but also about how you do it.

How you come across to others is a reflection
of your thoughts about yourself.

If you are not going to look out
for your well-being, who will?

Practice curiosity and beckon
the learner's heart.

Living by your values sets the tone
for your leadership.

Leadership is a paradox;
it provides structure but allows freedom.

Leadership is not about self-promotion;
it is about selfless service.

Leadership is rooted in love.

Recognize when to stop breakdowns
and realize how to start breakthroughs.

Low commitment has a high cost.

Do what you do, but do it in the best way
that you can.

OPEN YOUR

HEART,

NO MATTER

HOW MANY TIMES

FEAR HAS CLOSED IT.

To influence you must first connect.

You are stronger than you think,
wiser than you can imagine, and more powerful
than you have ever dreamed.

High expectation promotes excellence.

No matter how talented you are,
you still cannot do it all.

Leadership is a way to not only metabolize life,
but also to alchemize it.

Say yes to challenge and go and face it.

If those you lead sense a match
between your expectations of them
and your expectations of yourself,
they will follow your lead toward greatness.

Anticipate the needs of others.

Find ways to continuously develop
and grow talent.

See the invisible, believe the incredible,
and do the impossible.

Find purpose in your work
and meaning in your life.

Say yes to collaboration and no to competition.

Be a defender of what is important.

Allow people to connect to something bigger
than themselves at work.

If you can influence this moment,
you influence the future.

Focus on the root cause and not the quick fix.

THE
MORE
YOU
CLEAR
AWAY
THE
OUTSIDE

the more you remain open from the inside.

Knowing what is right is great.
Doing what is right is even better.

A helping hand is a helping heart.

If you think you have all the answers, you will
not be open to learning something new.

We work for people, not companies.

Think together, work together, feel together,
and make progress together.

To inspire others to excellence,
strive for nothing less than for yourself.

Evaluate where you are going and then
set your sights higher.

Heart, not money, is the real business capital.

Take full responsibility for your life,
starting right now.

Learning and having heart
are the mother of leadership.

Embrace your problems as gifts; view your
problems as the next steps for growth.

Make what matters really matter.

What gets celebrated — gets repeated.

Leadership is about unlocking the potential
of another to become better
than they think they are.

Performance without passion
is heart without purpose.

Start with what is important and urgent,
then do what is important but not urgent.

I am not my past.

I am what I choose to be

RIGHT
NOW.

Recognize when to stop informing
and realize when to start inspiring.

Say *yes* to life and *no* to struggle.

Accept responsibility for your feelings.

Know that there is something inside you
greater than any obstacle.

When you judge another,
you do not define them,
you define yourself.

Believe in yourself and all that you are.

We thrive from love; we survive from fear.

We cannot control what happens to us,
but we can control what we do next.

Learn to be smarter on how to be smarter.

There is no defeat except from within,
no insurmountable barrier except
our own inherent weakness of reason.

Everyone has the power to inspire
and change the world.

Promise nothing to others; just do
what you most enjoy doing.
In this way, you will always overdeliver!

Wherever you go, go with all your

HEART.

acknowledgements

I feel a deep gratitude for the generous help of friends and colleagues who enabled me to transform *Thoughts Spoken from the Heart* from a passionate idea into reality.

May all these wonderful gardeners who nurtured, watered, and blessed my project along the way see first-hand that it creates meaning for people in the world.

I wish to thank Frank Sonnenberg, my brilliant mentor and friend, who shared his vision and painstakingly stewarded the concept of this book from idea to completion with a generous and grateful heart. Frank's deep wisdom and unflagging sense of knowledge and thoughtfulness continuously call me back to my purpose.

Without Donna Spencer's editing magic none of this would be possible. I am extremely fortunate to work with Donna, who skillfully directs and prunes my work and makes me feel supported.

Carrie Ralston took my vision and made it visually beautiful. She knew the design of my heart and made it happen.

My beloved daughter, Michaela Katz, who stands by me through the dark and light. She supports, guides, listens, and nurtures me through all things that call upon us in life.

My beloved son, Ariel Katz, who is honest and minces no words about what he likes or dislikes — and so when he says he likes something, I know it must be good.

And my beloved daughter, Zoe Katz, who reminds me that to be human is not to be perfect, but to bring heart to all that you do. I love her with all my heart.

I am blessed, honored, and grateful to call you my children, and to call myself your mother. I love you unconditionally.

There are many dear friends I'd like to deeply thank: Becky Robinson, Jesse Lyn Stoner, Chris Edmonds, Julie Winkle, Wendy Appeal, Jacqueline Voncken, Cali Yost, Barbara Kimmel, Dan Oestreich, John Paul Anderson, Debbie Slater, Fran Held, Josh Getzler, Martina McGowan, Terri Klass, Sean Gardner, Alli Polin, Caron Sonnenberg, Blair Glaser, Lauren Yvonne White, Wally Bock, Emanuella, Chantal Bechervaise, Simon Harvey, Karin Hurt, Edwin Witvoet, Greg Richardson, Daniel Buhr, Pat Robeck, Peg Gilliard, Jandis Price, Terri Klass, Garren Fagaragan, Tracy Williams, Sharon Reed, Panteli Tritchew, Emelia Sam, and all of the loyal heart-based leaders at the #leadfromwithin community.

Last but not least, I want to thank you — you who have taken precious moments from your lives to stop and read my thoughts and comment, support, and share your heart with me. This is for you, in gratitude for your encouragement, compassion, and grace. I am honored to be walking this path with you.

My heart is dedicated to your heart.

about lolly

Lolly Daskal is a Leadership Global Consultant and Coach who is dedicated to helping cultivate the right values, vision, and culture for individuals and organizations. She is the founder of *Lead from Within*, a global consultancy whose clients range from heads of state and CEOs of large multinational companies to budding entrepreneurs.

Lolly's coaching, consulting, and speaking uses a heart-based leadership approach designed to help people achieve their full potential to make a difference in the world. The *Huffington Post* named Lolly one of its Most Inspiring Women in the World, and *Trust Across America* has recognized her as one of the Top 100 Thought Leaders in Trustworthy Business Behavior.

You can visit Lolly's website and blog at LollyDaskal.com or follow her on Twitter at @LollyDaskal.

Her weekly global *Lead from Within* tweetchat, in which she discusses emerging and important leadership topics of our time, engages with a Twitter community of over 4.5 million people every week.

Contact Info

Website   www.lollydaskal.com/
Twitter   twitter.com/LollyDaskal
LinkedIn www.linkedin.com/in/lollydaskal